StartUp Reading 3

Gina Kim and Carolyn S. Hyatt

WorldCom Edu

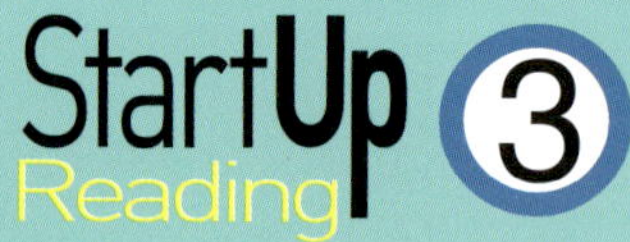

StartUp Reading 3

Gina Kim and Carolyn S. Hyatt

© 2006 published by WorldCom Edu.

Cover/Interior Design: Design Nalgae
Illustrations: Wishing Star

ISBN: 89-8127-621-8

Desk Copy Request / Information
To place your desk copy request or for more information, please contact the following office:
Tel: (02)3273-4300   Fax: (02)3273-4303
Homepage : www.wcbooks.co.kr

Contents

1. Special Trucks ·················· 4

2. Recycling Paper ·················· 8

3. Interesting People ·················· 12

4. Going to Town ·················· 16

5. Brave People ·················· 20

6. Something About Nature ·········· 24

7. The Stars and Stripes ············· 28

8. America's Most Famous House ··· 32

9. A Long Time Ago ················· 36

10. The Changing Ocean ············· 40

11. All About Trees ················· 44

12. Growing Up ·················· 48

1 Special Trucks

✳ Before You Read

1. Do you like cars?
2. Have you ever seen a monster truck?
3. How big is a monster truck?

Monster trucks are special trucks. They have big tires. There are different kinds of monster trucks. Some monster trucks are very long. Some are very wide. People use monster trucks for different reasons. They are very useful to people. Some people use the trucks to make **roads**. Others use them to **entertain** people. One **colorful** monster truck is called a fire truck. People use such trucks to put out fires. So, monster trucks help people a lot.

✳ Word Match

Match each word with the correct meaning.

1. **monster**	a. a large vehicle used for carrying heavy things
2. **road**	b. to make people laugh and smile
3. **truck**	c. a path for cars and people to travel on
4. **colorful**	d. having different colors
5. **entertain**	e. a large and scary living thing

✳ Reading Comprehension

Choose the best answer.

1. This story is about ________ .

    a. monsters   b. tires   c. monster trucks

2. Monster trucks have big ________ .

    a. tires   b. teeth   c. arms

3. Some monster trucks are very ________ .

    a. wide   b. narrow   c. thin

4. You can tell that monster trucks are never ________ .

    a. long   b. small   c. wide

✳ General Understanding

Circle T for true or F for false.

1. Monster trucks have small tires.   T   F

2. All monster trucks look the same.   T   F

3. Some monster trucks are very long.   T   F

4. A fire truck is colorful.   T   F

✳ Word Practice

A Circle the correct word.

1. Monster _______ are fun to drive.　　　[horses ǀ trucks]

2. A giraffe has a _______ neck.　　　[short ǀ long]

3. I like rainbows. They are _______.　　　[colorful ǀ blue]

4. Can I _______ your pen?　　　[use ǀ shoes]

5. The sea is very deep and _______.　　　[tall ǀ wide]

B Choose the right word from the box below.

monster	long	useful	roads

1. _______ trucks have big tires.

2. Some people use the trucks to make _______.

3. Some monster trucks are very _______.

4. Monster trucks are _______ to people.

✳ Picture Comprehension

Circle the picture of a fire truck.

a   b   c   d

✳ Summary & Listening Practice

SUR3-1-02
MP3

Monster ①________ have big tires. Monster trucks are very
②________ to people. People ③________ them for many things.
A fire truck is also a ④________ truck. It is very ⑤________.

2 Recycling Paper

✳ Before You Read

1. Do you like to make things with paper?
2. What can you make with paper?
3. Do you have any old paper at home?

People cut down many trees to make paper.
We can help **save** the trees. People throw away old paper.
But we can use it to make new paper. You put the old paper
into a big box. Then you put the box outside. Some workers
come and take the box. The box is taken to a special
building. A machine **cuts** the old paper into little **pieces**.
They **join** together to become new paper. In this way, we can
save lots and lots of trees. Quite a good idea, isn't it?

✳ Word Match

Match each word with the correct meaning.

1. **save**		a.	a bit or part of something
2. **building**		b.	to divide something into parts
3. **join**		c.	anything built to do things in
4. **cut**		d.	to help something or someone
5. **piece**		e.	to put two things together

✳ Reading Comprehension

Choose the best answer.

1. This story is about making old paper ________.

   a. nice　　　　b. new　　　　c. big

2. People cut down many ________ to make paper.

   a. trees　　　　b. boxes　　　　c. machines

3. The box with the old paper is put ________.

   a. inside　　　　b. outside　　　　c. in the trees

4. You have to cut the old paper into little ________ before it becomes new paper.

   a. squares　　　　b. circles　　　　c. pieces

✳ General Understanding

Circle T for true or F for false.

1. People cut down many trees.　　　　T　F

2. People throw away new paper.　　　　T　F

3. Some workers come and take the box of old paper.　　　　T　F

4. A machine cuts the old paper into pieces.　　　　T　F

 Word Practice

A Circle the correct word.

1. It is very cold and dark ________. [outside | on]

2. Don't drink the milk. ________ it away. [Sing | Throw]

3. I ________ my hair myself. [cut | but]

4. I want a ________ of cake. [piece | peace]

5. Where did I ________ my glasses? [paint | put]

B Choose the right word from the box below.

building	save	put	use

1. We can ________ trees.

2. We can ________ old paper to make new paper.

3. ________ the old paper into a box.

4. Some workers take the box to a ________.

✳ Picture Comprehension

Choose the picture that goes with the sentence.

Circle the picture of a man cutting a tree.

a   b   c   d

✳ Summary & Listening Practice

SUR3-2-04
MP3

Listen and fill in the blanks.

We put old paper ①＿＿＿＿ a box to make new paper. The box is taken to a special ②＿＿＿＿. A machine then ③＿＿＿＿ up the old paper into ④＿＿＿＿. The pieces then become new paper. In this way, we can ⑤＿＿＿＿ many trees.

3 Interesting People

✳ Before You Read

1. Do you like cowboys?
2. What kind of clothes do cowboys wear?
3. Do you know where cowboys live?

You can still see some cowboys today. Cowboys live on a **ranch**. They look after cattle and they ride horses. They wake up **early** in the morning. They **wear** big hats and boots with pointed toes. Cowboys also wear jeans most of the time. Some of them have leather pant legs on. These leather pant legs are called chaps. Cowboys put on chaps when they go through **sharp bushes**. Wow, they live very interesting lives. How about meeting some cowboys this weekend?

✳ Word Match

Match each word with the correct meaning.

1. **ranch**   a. a plant with many woody branches

2. **bush**   b. a large farm

3. **sharp**   c. near the beginning

4. **early**   d. to have on the body

5. **wear**   e. having a thin edge

✳ Reading Comprehension

Choose the best answer.

1. This story is about _______ .

    a. cowboys　　　b. cows　　　c. a ranch

2. Cowboys live on a _______ .

    a. horse　　　b. beach　　　c. ranch

3. Cowboys like to wear _______ .

    a. skirts　　　b. jeans　　　c. shorts

4. You can tell that cowboys work around _______ .

    a. cities　　　b. pigs　　　c. bushes

✳ General Understanding

Circle T for true or F for false.

1. Cowboys live on a large farm.　　　T　F

2. They look after bugs.　　　T　F

3. Cowboys wear big glasses.　　　T　F

4. Some cowboys put on leather pant legs.　　　T　F

✳ Word Practice

A Circle the correct word.

1. I don't like going bed too _______ .   [early | curly]

2. Be careful. That knife is very _______ .   [stay | sharp]

3. I like to _______ my red dress.   [wear | win]

4. _______ me up at 7 a.m.   [Wake | Fake]

5. Can you _______ a horse?   [write | ride]

B Choose the right word from the box below.

wear	early	have	ride

1. Some cowboys _______ leather pant legs on.

2. Cowboys _______ horses.

3. They wake up _______ in the morning.

4. They _______ boots with pointed toes.

✳ Picture Comprehension

Choose the picture that goes with the sentence.

Circle the picture of a cowboy riding a horse.

a

b

c

d

✳ Summary & Listening Practice

SUR3-3-06
MP3

Listen and fill in the blanks.

Cowboys live on a ①________. They wake up ②________ every day.
They wear ③________ and ④________. They also wear leather pant
legs called chaps. They wear chaps because bushes are ⑤________.

4 Going to Town

✳ Before You Read

1. Do you like cars?
2. What kind of car do your parents drive?
3. Which do you like better, walking or driving in a car?

A long time ago, there were no roads. Animals left footprints on the ground. At first, people followed animal footprints. Later, they started to make their own **paths**. Then people **invented** carts and started to **build** roads. They made roads with **bricks**. The roads were very strong. Many roads were built from one town to another. Then cars were made to **drive** on those roads. You can see many cars and roads today. They help you move very fast. So cars and roads are very important.

✳ Word Match

Match each word with the correct meaning.

1. **invent**   a. a block used for building
2. **drive**   b. to control cars or other vehicles
3. **path**   c. to make something
4. **brick**   d. to make something never made before
5. **build**   e. a narrow road for walking on

✳ Reading Comprehension

Choose the best answer.

1. This story is about ________.

   a. animals   b. roads   c. footprints

2. At first, men followed ________ footprints.

   a. animal   b. cart   c. brick

3. Later, people invented ________.

   a. animals   b. footprints   c. carts

4. You can tell that a long time ago, people did not have ________.

   a. horses   b. carts   c. parents

✳ General Understanding

Circle T for true or F for false.

1. A long time ago, there were many roads.   T F

2. Some time later, people built houses.   T F

3. People made roads with bricks.   T F

4. The roads were not strong.   T F

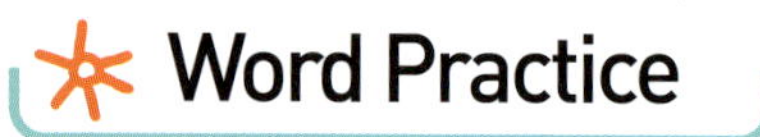 Word Practice

A Circle the correct word.

1. It is difficult to _______ a house. [build | sleep]

2. There are _______ trees in a forest. [many | ago]

3. It is difficult to _______ when it rains. [drink | drive]

4. Tom can lift heavy boxes. He is very _______.

   [weak | strong]

5. I build houses with _______. [bricks | tricks]

B Choose the right word from the box below.

build	strong	paths	drive

1. Long ago people first made their own _______.

2. People started to _______ roads.

3. People made _______ roads with bricks.

4. Cars were invented for people to _______.

✳ Picture Comprehension

Choose the picture that goes with the sentence.

Circle the picture of men building a road.

a   b   c   d

✳ Summary & Listening Practice

Listen and fill in the blanks.

A long time ago, there were no ①________. People followed animal footprints. Later, they made their own ②________. Then they started to ③________ roads with ④________. They invented cars to ⑤________ on those roads. You can see many cars and roads today.

 Brave People

 Before You Read

1. What is a knight?
2. What kind of clothes did knights wear?
3. Did knights ride horses?

Do you know about knights? They wore **iron suits** and rode horses. Only those boys whose fathers were noblemen became knights. Such fathers taught their sons to be kind, **brave** and strong. When a boy turned 15, he left home. He worked for another knight. When he turned 21, he became a knight. Knights wore iron suits to **protect** themselves. So they could fight bravely in **battle**. Knights were very brave people.

Word Match

Match each word with the correct meaning.

1. **suit**   a. a fight during a war

2. **brave**   b. a formal set of clothes

3. **battle**   c. to keep someone from being hurt

4. **iron**   d. ready to face pain or danger

5. **protect**   e. a strong heavy metal

✳ Reading Comprehension

Choose the best answer.

1. This story is about _______.

   a. horses   b. boys   c. knights

2. Knights rode _______.

   a. camels   b. horses   c. elephants

3. Knights wore _______ to protect themselves.

   a. iron suits   b. leather jackets   c. wood suits

4. You can tell that not everyone could become a _______.

   a. knight   b. father   c. boy

✳ General Understanding

Circle T for true or F for false.

1. Knights rode horses.   T   F

2. All boys became knights.   T   F

3. Knights wore leather suits.   T   F

4. Knights didn't fight in battle.   T   F

✳ Word Practice

A Circle the correct word.

1. Lions are _______ animals.   [brave | weak]

2. My father has _______ arms.   [cry | strong]

3. I can _______ a horse.   [ride | run]

4. Birds_______ themselves with their beaks.   [do | protect]

5. I like to _______ my red dress.   [win | wear]

B Choose the right word from the box below.

brave	iron	fight	knights

1. _______ were soldiers who wore iron suits.

2. Knights were _______ and strong.

3. Knights wore _______ suits.

4. Knights could _______ bravely.

✳ Picture Comprehension

Choose the picture that goes with the sentence.

Circle the picture of a knight.

a

b

c

d

✳ Summary & Listening Practice

SUR3-5-10
MP3

Listen and fill in the blanks.

Only some ①_______ could become knights. Boys were taught to be kind and ②_______. Knights wore ③_______ suits and rode horses. Iron suits could ④_______ knights because they were strong. Knights fought bravely in ⑤_______.

6 Something About Nature

✳ Before You Read

1. Name the four seasons.
2. What is your favorite season?
3. In which season do you see snow?

The four seasons are spring, summer, autumn and winter. In the spring, the cold air goes away. All the leaves turn green and flowers **bloom**. In the summer, it is very hot. Fruits begin to **ripen**. In the autumn, leaves **change** color. People get ready for cold **weather**. In the winter, you can see snow. Many animals stay inside because it is cold outside. Everything is **quiet**. Every season has something special. What is your favorite season?

✳ Word Match

Match each word with the correct meaning.

1. **change**	a.	to produce flowers
2. **bloom**	b.	with little or no noise
3. **ripen**	c.	the conditions outside
4. **weather**	d.	to become different
5. **quiet**	e.	to become ready to be eaten

⁎ Reading Comprehension

Choose the best answer.

1. This story is about _______.

   a. the four seasons   b. flowers   c. winter

2. Leaves change color in the _______.

   a. autumn   b. summer   c. winter

3. In the winter, you can see _______.

   a. flowers   b. fruits   c. snow

4. You can tell that you don't see animals in the _______.

   a. autumn   b. winter   c. spring

⁎ General Understanding

Circle T for true or F for false.

1. You can eat many fruits in the spring.   T   F

2. Leaves turn green in the spring.   T   F

3. In the summer, it is very hot.   T   F

4. In the winter, you can see flowers outside.   T   F

Word Practice

A Circle the correct word.

1. Every summer, fruits begin to ________ .   [ripen | pipe]

2. The road is icy. It is very ________ today.   [cold | hot]

3. Be ________ . Don't wake the babies up.   [noisy | quiet]

4. When flowers ________ , they smell nice.   [blame | bloom]

5. It is raining ________ .   [outside | inside]

B Choose the right word from the box below.

change	spring	ripen	winter

1. Flowers bloom in the ________ .

2. Fruits begin to ________ in the summer.

3. Leaves ________ color in the autumn.

4. You can see snow in the ________ .

✳ Picture Comprehension

Choose the picture that goes with the sentence.

Circle the picture of autumn.

a

b

c

d

✳ Summary & Listening Practice

Listen and fill in the blanks.

SUR3-6-12
MP3

There are four ①________.
Flowers ②________ in the
spring. Fruits begin to
③________ in the summer. In
the autumn, you should get
ready for cold ④________. It
snows in the winter.
Everything is ⑤________ in the
winter. I like all four seasons.

7 The Stars and Stripes

✳ Before You Read

1. How many colors does your country's flag have?
2. Does your country's flag have any stars?
3. How many country flags do you know?

Every country has its **own** flag. All the flags are different. Let's look at the American flag. It is over 200 years old. It is red, white and blue. It also has 13 red and white **stripes**. The upper corner of the flag has fifty white stars. Each star **represents** a **state**. The American flag has special meaning for all Americans. They are very **proud** of it. The American flag is also called the Stars and Stripes.

✳ Word Match

Match each word with the correct meaning.

1. **own**   a. to stand for
2. **proud**   b. a line or long, narrow section
3. **stripe**   c. feeling pleased and worthy
4. **represent**   d. a political part of a nation
5. **state**   e. belonging to oneself alone

✳ Reading Comprehension

Choose the best answer.

1. This story is about ________ .

   a. flags   b. the American flag   c. stars

2. Every country has its own ________ .

   a. flag   b. language   c. air

3. The American flag has 13 red and white ________ .

   a. colors   b. shapes   c. stripes

4. You can tell that no two countries have the same ________ .

   a. flag   b. language   c. air

✳ General Understanding

Circle T for true or F for false.

1. All flags are the same.   T   F

2. The American flag is over 200 years old.   T   F

3. The American flag has 13 red and white stripes.   T   F

4. The upper corner of the American flag has   T   F

   40 red stars.

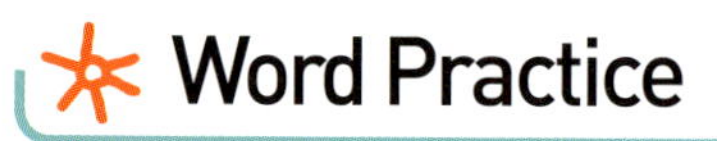 **Word Practice**

A Circle the correct word.

1. I bought this book with my _______ money.

[own | town]

2. This is a very _______ book. Some pages are missing.

[new | old]

3. Zebras have black and white _______. [dots | stripes]

4. It is in the left _______. [corner | happy]

5. There are 50 _______ in America. [states | buildings]

B Choose the right word from the box below.

old	stripes	own	corner

1. Every country has its _______ flag.

2. The American flag is very _______.

3. It has red and white _______.

4. In the _______, there are 50 stars.

✳ Picture Comprehension

Choose the picture that goes with the sentence.

Circle the picture of the American flag.

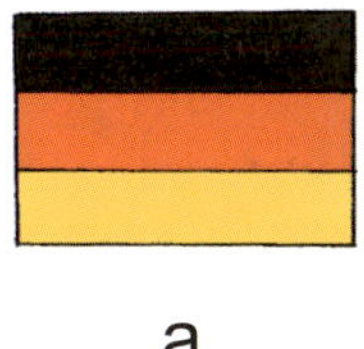

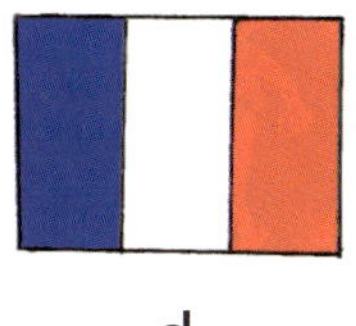

a   b   c   d

✳ Summary & Listening Practice

Listen and fill in the blanks.

SUR3-7-14
MP3

The American flag is ①________ 200 years old. It has 13 ②________.
In the upper ③________, it has 50 stars. There are 50 ④________ in
America. Each star represents a state. Americans are very
⑤________ of the American flag.

8 America's Most Famous House

✳ Before You Read

1. Do you know who lives in the White House?
2. Have you ever seen a picture of the White House?
3. Why is it called the White House?

The **President** of the United States of America lives in the White House. You can see the White House in Washington D.C. Policemen **always** stand by the door to the White House. They **guard** it day and night. There are three **floors** in the White House. The first floor is for the President to work. The other two floors are for the President and his family to live. They love their country and its people very **much**. And they are proud of the White House.

✳ Word Match

Match each word with the correct meaning.

1. **guard**		a.	all the time
2. **floor**		b.	to watch over something
3. **always**		c.	to a great degree
4. **president**		d.	a level of a building
5. **much**		e.	a leader of a group or nation

✳ Reading Comprehension

Choose the best answer.

1. This story is about _______.

   a. policemen   b. guards   c. the White House

2. The White House is in _______.

   a. Florida   b. New York   c. Washington D.C.

3. The White House has _______ floors.

   a. three   b. four   c. five

4. You can tell that only special people can visit the _______.

   a. White House   b. policemen   c. United States of America

✳ General Understanding

Circle T for true or F for false.

1. The White House is in Washington D.C.   T   F

2. Policemen always stand by the door of the
   White House.   T   F

3. There are four floors in the White House.   T   F

4. The President and his family live on the first floor.   T   F

 Word Practice

A Circle the correct word.

1. My dogs _______ my house all the time.

[guard | bored]

2. It's _______ hot in Africa.   [sometimes | always]

3. Three _______ caught the bank robbers.

[policemen | ants]

4. I love music so _______.   [many | much]

5. We have to _______. There are no seats left.

[sit | stand]

B Choose the right word from the box below.

floors	guard	stand	President

1. Policemen _______ the door day and night.

2. Policemen always _______ by the door to the White House.

3. There are three _______ in the White House.

4. The _______ lives in the White House.

 Picture Comprehension

Choose the picture that goes with the sentence.

Circle the picture of the White House.

a

b

c

d

 Summary & Listening Practice

Listen and fill in the blanks.

SUR3-8-16
MP3

The White House is in Washington D.C. The ①________ of the United States of America ②________ in the White House. There are ③________ many ④________ outside the White House. The White House has three ⑤________ .

9 A Long Time Ago

✳ Before You Read

1. What kind of food do you like to eat?
2. Do you like to eat Western food?
3. Do you like to eat vegetables?

A long time ago, people **hunted** for food. They found berries and roots. They also killed wild animals. They didn't cook food. Instead they ate all the food **raw**. After some time, fire was **discovered**. People used it to cook food. After that, people learned how to **raise** animals. Some people became farmers. Towns began to grow and there were more people to feed. So people started to look for better ways to get food. There were many ways of getting food. Do you know what people **decided** to do?

✳ Word Match

Match each word with the correct meaning.

1. **hunt**   a. to make a choice
2. **decide**   b. not cooked
3. **raw**   c. to find before anyone else
4. **raise**   d. to try to find and kill
5. **discover**   e. to take care of animals

✳ Reading Comprehension

Choose the best answer.

1. This story is about _______ .

    a. hunters   b. getting food   c. berries

2. In the early days, people killed wild _______ .

    a. animals   b. berries   c. plants

3. After some time, people used _______ to cook food.

    a. stove   b. pot   c. fire

4. You can tell that a long time ago, people did not cook _______ .

    a. plants   b. towns   c. food

✳ General Understanding

Circle T for true or F for false.

1. Long ago, people did not hunt for food.   T   F

2. In the early days, people did not cook their food.   T   F

3. People used fire to cook food in the past.   T   F

4. People began to raise animals a long time ago.   T   F

✳ Word Practice

A Circle the correct word.

1. Pigs live on a _______.   [sea | farm]

2. Some people still _______ for food.   [hunt | begin]

3. I _______ to learn English.   [happy | decided]

4. I hate eating _______ fish.   [raw | early]

5. My dad likes to _______ for us.   [took | cook]

B Choose the right word from the box below.

raw	hunted	raise	cook

1. A long time ago, people _______ for food.

2. They ate their food _______.

3. They used fire to _______ food.

4. They started to _______ animals.

✳ Picture Comprehension

Choose the picture that goes with the sentence.

Circle the picture of the people cooking food.

a   b   c   d

✳ Summary & Listening Practice

SUR3-9-18
MP3

Listen and fill in the blanks.

People ① _______ for food a long time ago. ② _______ that, they started to ③ _______ animals. Towns got bigger and there were more ④ _______ to feed. They ⑤ _______ to find other ways to get food.

10 The Changing Ocean

✳ Before You Read

1. Do you like to go to the ocean?
2. Do you like to swim in the ocean?
3. When can you swim in the ocean?

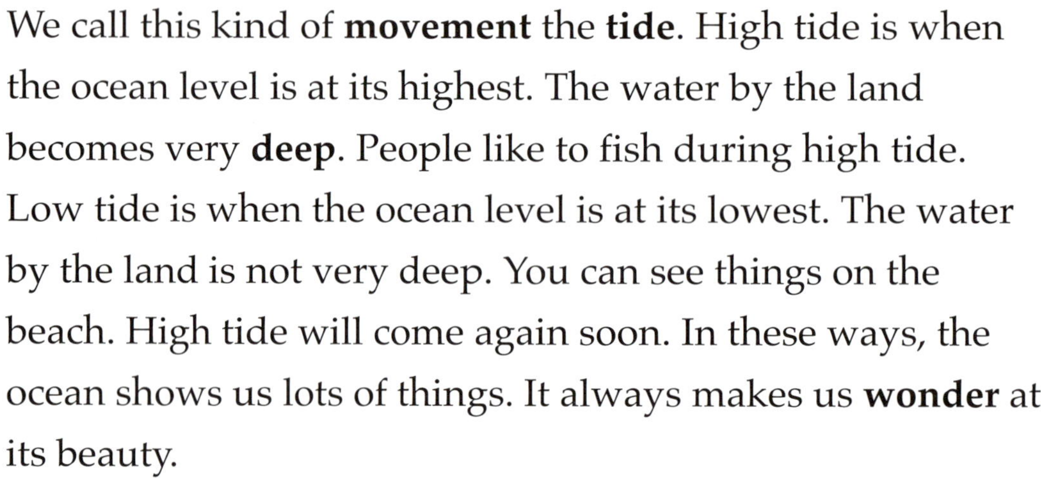

The level of the **ocean** changes all the time.
We call this kind of **movement** the **tide**. High tide is when
the ocean level is at its highest. The water by the land
becomes very **deep**. People like to fish during high tide.
Low tide is when the ocean level is at its lowest. The water
by the land is not very deep. You can see things on the
beach. High tide will come again soon. In these ways, the
ocean shows us lots of things. It always makes us **wonder** at
its beauty.

✳ Word Match

Match each word with the correct meaning.

1. **movement**   a. the largest bodies of water on the earth

2. **tide**   b. something that changes position

3. **ocean**   c. the change in the level of the sea or ocean

4. **deep**   d. to feel surprise

5. **wonder**   e. going down a long way

✳ Reading Comprehension

Choose the best answer.

1. The story is about _______.

   a. tides   b. the ocean   c. swimming

2. The ocean changes _______.

   a. at night   b. in the winter   c. all the time

3. During low tide, you can see many things on the _______.

   a. trees   b. beach   c. tides

4. You can tell that you can only fish during _______.

   a. high tide   b. low tide   c. the rainy season

✳ General Understanding

Circle T for true or F for false.

1. The ocean changes out only at night.   T   F

2. The level of the ocean never changes.   T   F

3. During high tide, the water becomes deep.   T   F

4. People like to fish during low tide.   T   F

✳ Word Practice

A Circle the correct word.

1. The rainy season will _________ soon.   [come ┃ call]

2. Be careful, the sea is very _________.   [deep ┃ dive]

3. I _________ why she likes me.   [thunder ┃ wonder]

4. Whales live in the _________.   [sky ┃ ocean]

5. Elephants _________ very slowly.   [move ┃ make]

B Choose the right word from the box below.

ocean	tide	deep	moves

1. The ocean _________ all the time.

2. High tide is when the _________ level is at its highest.

3. The water by the land is not _________ during low tide.

4. People like to fish during high _________.

 Picture Comprehension

Circle the picture of low tide.

a   b   c   d

Summary & Listening Practice

Listen and fill in the blanks.

The ①_______ level is always changing. We call this ②_______ the tide. The water by the land is ③_______ during high tide. During low ④_______, the water by the land is not very deep. Every time I see tides, I ⑤_______ how special they are.

11 All About Trees

* Before You Read

1. Do you like trees?
2. Do you like to climb trees?
3. What kind of tree do you like?

A tree has five main parts. Each part has a special job. The **roots** hold water and **store** food. The trunk **sends** water up to the leaves. It also sends food down to the roots. The branches keep the twigs in place. The **bark** covers the tree on the outside and looks after it. The **buds** are also very important. The leaves come from them. All the parts have many different jobs. So they help each other.

* Word Match

Match each word with the correct meaning.

1. **bud**   a. to keep for future use

2. **root**   b. the outside of plants

3. **store**   c. to make something go to another place

4. **send**   d. a part of plants that grows underground

5. **bark**   e. a small lump on trees that grows into new leaves or flowers

✳ Reading Comprehension

Choose the best answer.

1. This story is about ________.

   a. leaves   b. flowers   c. tree parts

2. The ________ hold water and store food.

   a. leaves   b. branches   c. roots

3. The trunk sends ________ up to the leaves.

   a. food   b. water   c. sunlight

4. You can tell that each part of the tree is very ________.

   a. big   b. important   c. small

✳ General Understanding

Circle T for true or F for false.

1. A tree has four main parts.   T   F

2. Each part has a special job.   T   F

3. The branches hold water.   T   F

4. The bark covers the tree.   T   F

✳ Word Practice

A Circle the correct word.

1. Tim _______ me a letter every week.　　[sends | sees]

2. Leaves come from the _______.　　[buds | birds]

3. Where do you _______ your English books?

　　[keep | kind]

4. Where can I _______ my books?　　[stop | store]

5. The blanket _______ us. It keeps us warm.　　[covers | comes]

B Choose the right word from the box below.

sends	bark	roots	keep

1. The _______ store food.

2. The trunk _______ water up to the leaves.

3. The branches _______ the twigs in place.

4. The _______ covers the tree on the outside.

✳ Picture Comprehension

Choose the picture that goes with the sentence.

Circle the picture of a tree.

a　　　　　b　　　　　c　　　　　d

✳ Summary & Listening Practice

Listen and fill in the blanks.

SUR3-11-22
MP3

A tree has five main parts. The
①________ hold water and
②________ food. The ③________
looks after the tree on the
outside of it. The trunk ④________
water up to the leaves. The
branches and ⑤________ have
special jobs, too.

12 Growing Up

* Before You Read

1. What does a seed look like?
2. What color are seeds?
3. How big are seeds?

Seeds have different **sizes**. Some are big and others are small. Some seeds grow **quickly**. Others grow **slowly**. Seeds start to grow when they get water. Wind and water sometimes **carry** seeds to other places. Sometimes animals eat some of the seeds that fall on the ground. Seeds must have water and sunlight to grow. So water and sunlight help them in many ways. With their help, seeds become stronger.

* Word Match

Match each word with the correct meaning.

1. **size**   a. a small thing made by plants that grows into a new plant

2. **quickly**   b. at a slow speed

3. **slowly**   c. fast or hurriedly

4. **carry**   d. how big or small something is

5. **seed**   e. to hold something while moving

✳ Reading Comprehension

Choose the best answer.

1. This story is about ________.

    a. seeds   b. wind   c. water

2. Seeds start to grow when they get ________.

    a. sun   b. water   c. wind

3. Sometimes ________ eat seeds.

    a. flowers   b. plants   c. animals

4. You can tell that seeds need ________ or water to move.

    a. wind   b. sun   c. ground

✳ General Understanding

Circle T for true or F for false.

1. Some seeds grow quickly.   T   F

2. All seeds are the same.   T   F

3. Seeds need water to grow.   T   F

4. Animals cannot eat seeds.   T   F

✳ Word Practice

A Circle the correct word.

1. Snails move _______ .   [quickly | slowly]

2. Help me _______ these boxes.   [carry | cherry]

3. Trains move very _______ .   [slowly | quickly]

4. I drink eight glasses of _______ every day. [water | bread]

5. Rabbits are _______ animals.   [small | big]

B Choose the right word from the box below.

small	carry	sizes	quickly

1. All seeds have different _______ .

2. Some seeds are big and others are _______ .

3. Some seeds grow _______ .

4. Wind can _______ seeds.

✳ Picture Comprehension

Choose the picture that goes with the sentence.

Circle the picture of the seeds.

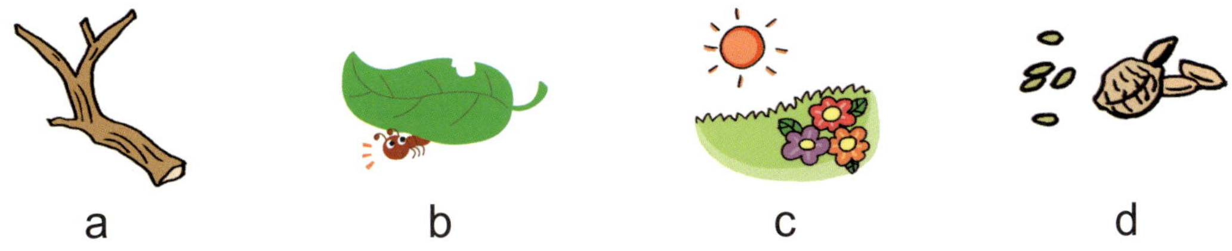

a   b   c   d

✳ Summary & Listening Practice

Listen and fill in the blanks.

SUR3-12-24
MP3

All ①_______ are different. They have different ②_______. Some are big and others are small. Some grow ③_______ and others grow ④_______. Wind and water ⑤_______ seeds to different places. They become new plants.

3

StartUp Reading

Workbook

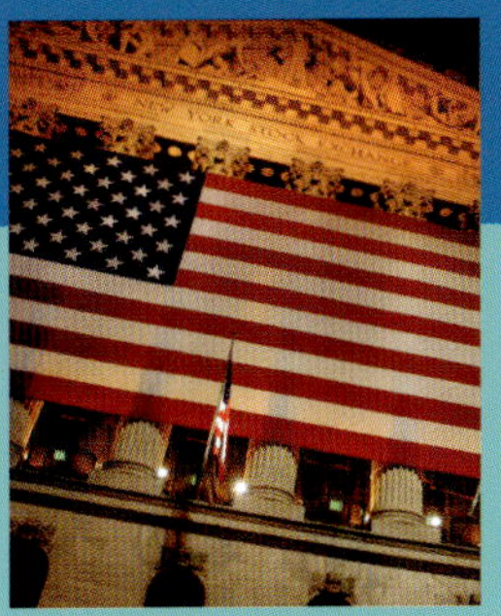

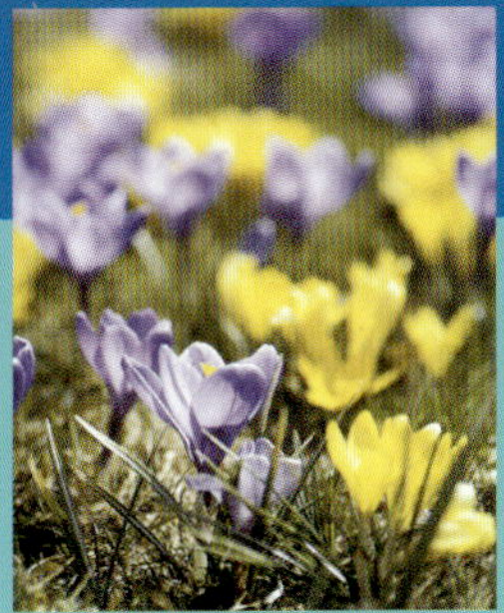

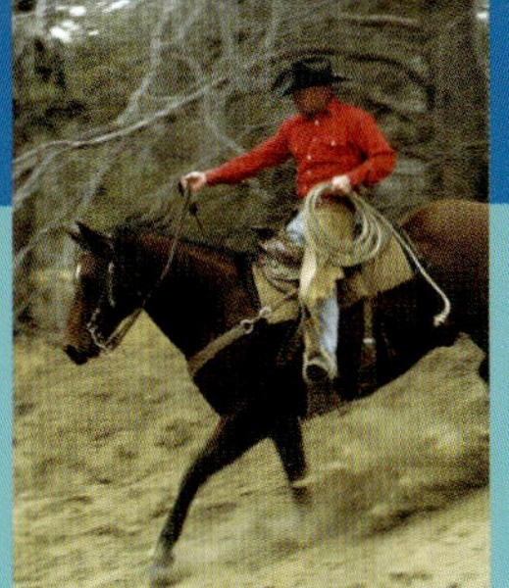

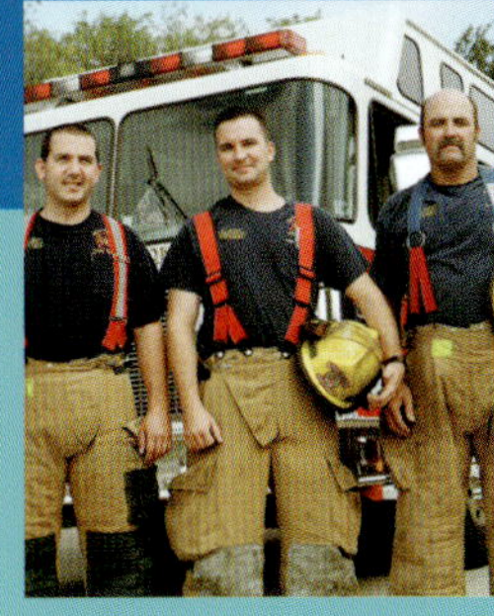

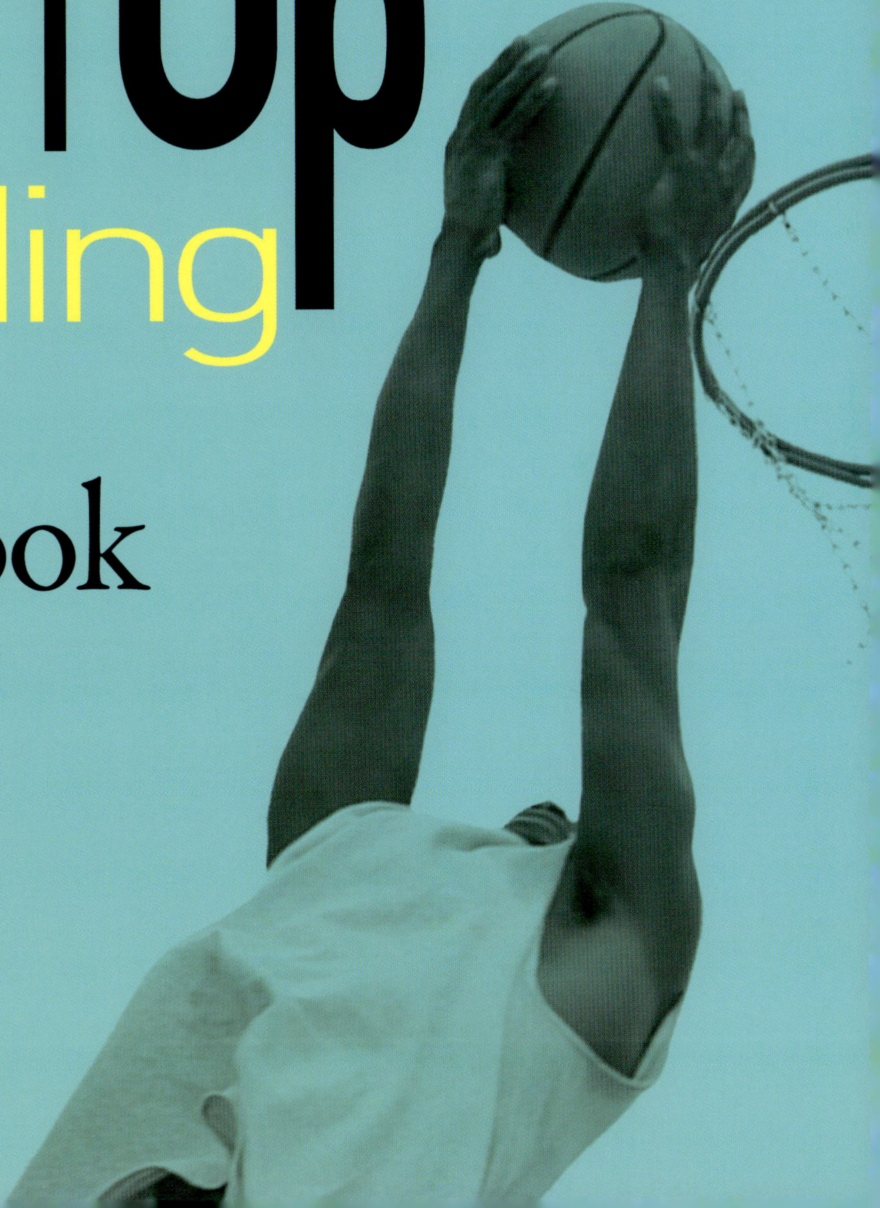

WorldCom Edu

✳ Vocabulary

New words to know

truck   *n.* a heavy vehicle used to carry goods
Ex. My father is a truck driver.

wide   *adj.* reaching across a large area from side to side
Ex. I walked through the wide doorway alone.

tire   *n.* the thick rubber ring that fits around the outside of a wheel
Ex. I have a flat tire.

monster   *n.* a creature that is large, ugly and frightening
Ex. She is afraid of monsters.

road   *n.* a path for cars and people to travel on
Ex. People built a new road.

carry   *v.* to take something from one place to another
Ex. I will carry your bag for you.

travel   *v.* to go from one place to another
Ex. She travels a lot on business.

colorful   *adj.* full of color
Ex. This is quite a colorful shirt.

scary   *adj.* frightening
Ex. It was a scary ghost story.

useful   *adj.* able to be used in a helpful way
Ex. I have a useful book that tells which food is good for health.

SUR3-1-01
MP3

⭐ Listening

A Listen to the dialog and choose the best answer. 🎵 WB 25

1. What is the conversation about?

   a. A small truck b. A monster truck

   c. A cute truck

2. What is true about the conversation?

   a. A monster truck is cute.

   b. A monster truck is small.

   c. A monster truck is big.

3. What is true about the boy?

   a. He knows what a monster truck is.

   b. He does not know what a monster truck is.

   c. He does not like monster trucks.

B Listen and write the words you hear. 🎵 WB 26

1. Monster __________ are special in __________ ways.

2. There are many different __________ of __________ trucks.

3. People __________ monster trucks __________ do lots of

   things.

4. Monster trucks __________ be used to put __________

   fires.

5. A fire truck is very __________ .

✳ Vocabulary Review

A What does the underlined word mean in each sentence?

1. Funny movies <u>entertain</u> us.
    a. make us laugh and smile   b. make us hungry
    c. make us sad

2. Wow, look at this <u>colorful</u> shirt!
    a. having many colors   b. having one color only
    c. having no color

B Choose the one word that best fits each sentence.

1. Everybody is very __________ .
    a. special   b. specially   c. specialness

2. Some use monster trucks to __________ out fires.
    a. puts   b. put   c. putting

3. Monster trucks are very __________ to people.
    a. useful   b. use   c. usefulness

✳ Writing

Put the words in the correct order.

1. trucks / special / trucks / are / Monster

    ____

2. monster / very / trucks / Some / long / are

    ____

3. to / people / They / very / are / useful

    ____

✳ Vocabulary

New words to know

recycle	*v.* to keep used materials and use them again *Ex. Don't throw away your bags. Recycle them.*
paper	*n.* a thin flat material that you use for writing *Ex. I need a piece of paper.*
cut down	to make something fall down *Ex. He cut down a tree.*
tree	*n.* a tall plant that can live for a long time *Ex. Look at the apple trees!*
save	*v.* to keep something or someone safe *Ex. You saved my life.*
throw away	to get rid of garbage *Ex. I will throw his letter away.*
new	*adj.* not known before; recently made *Ex. He is reading a new book.*
box	*n.* a container; something to put things into *Ex. A box often has a lid.*
piece	*n.* one of the parts *Ex. Give me a piece of cake, please.*
join	*v.* to put two things together *Ex. The two pieces of wood were carefully joined.*

 **Listening**

SUR3-2-03
MP3

A Listen to the dialog and choose the best answer. 📱 WB 27

1. What is the conversation about?

   a. Saving trees   b. Recycled paper

   c. New paper

2. What is true about the conversation?

   a. People use old paper to make recycled paper.

   b. People use new paper to make recycled paper.

   c. People use boxes to make recycled paper.

3. What is true about the girl?

   a. She does not like the boy.

   b. She does not believe the boy.

   c. She believes the boy.

B Listen and write the words you hear. 📱 WB 28

1. We can ____________ lots of trees.

2. Don't ____________ away ____________ paper.

3. Some workers ____________ old paper to a ____________ .

4. A machine can ____________ paper into ____________ .

5. Old ____________ becomes ____________ paper.

✳ Vocabulary Review

A What does the underlined word mean in each sentence?

1. Can you <u>join</u> them?
    a. to put two things together
    b. to cut something into pieces
    c. to move something to a place

2. We can <u>save</u> a lot of trees by using recycled paper.
    a. to kill   b. to hurt   c. to help

B Choose the one word that best fits each sentence.

1. How can we help _____________ trees?
    a. save   b. saves   c. saving

2. _____________ the box outside.
    a. Puts   b. Put   c. Putting

3. They come and _____________ the paper.
    a. takes   b. take   c. taking

✳ Writing

Put the words in the correct order.

1. can / We / save / trees / the / help

   ____

2. paper / old / People / away / throw

   ____

3. you / the / put / Then / outside / box

   ____

✳ Vocabulary

New words to know

cowboy   *n.* a man who looks after cows and rides horses
Ex. I want to meet a cowboy.

ranch   *n.* a large farm
Ex. There are a lot of cows on this ranch.

today   *adv.* at the present time
Ex. Students today know very little about geography.

cattle   *n.* male and female cows
Ex. He looks after his cattle very well.

wake up   to stop sleeping
Ex. Wake up! It's nearly 8 o'clock!

early   *adv.* near the beginning; before the usual time
Ex. I get up early on weekday mornings.

morning   *n.* the early part of the day
Ex. Bye, see you in the morning.

wear   *v.* to have clothes on your body
Ex. He was wearing a suit and tie.

boot   *n.* a type of shoe that covers your foot and calf area
Ex. You need a new pair of ski boots.

leather   *n.* the skin of animals which has been treated
Ex. Leather is used to make shoes and bags.

SUR3-3-05
MP3

✳ Listening

A Listen to the dialog and choose the best answer.  **WB** 29

1. What is the conversation about?

   a. Cowboys   b. Girls   c. Horses

2. What is true about the conversation?

   a. Cowboys ride cows.

   b. Cowboys ride horses.

   c. Cowboys ride bikes.

3. What is true about the girl?

   a. She wants to be a cow.

   b. She wants to be a cowgirl.

   c. She wants to be a teacher.

B Listen and write the words you hear. **WB** 30

1. Cowboys live on a ___________ .

2. Cowboys wake up in __________ morning.

3. Cowboys like to __________ boots and __________ .

4. Cowboys __________ leather __________ legs on.

5. Cowboys go through sharp __________ .

✳ Vocabulary Review

A What does the underlined word mean in each sentence?

1. They live on a <u>ranch</u>.
    a. a small farm   b. a field   c. a large farm

2. Chris likes to <u>wear</u> jeans.
    a. to sit on   b. to stand on   c. to have on

B Choose the one word that best fits each sentence.

1. You can ___________ lots of birds there.
    a. sees   b. see   c. seeing

2. The boots have ___________ toes.
    a. points   b. pointed   c. pointing

3. The leather pant legs are ___________ chaps.
    a. called   b. call   c. calling

✳ Writing

Put the words in the correct order.

1. still / You / see / today / can / cowboys

    ____

2. a / live / Cowboys / ranch / on

    ____

3. ride / they / look / horses / after / cattle / They / and

    ____

✳ Vocabulary

New words to know

town	*n.* a place with many streets and buildings *Ex. A town is smaller than a city.*
own	*adj.* used to show something belongs to a person *Ex. I saw it with my own eyes.*
path	*n.* a way across a piece of land *Ex. There was a narrow path.*
cart	*n.* a vehicle with wheels used to transport things *Ex. I will bring a cart.*
vehicle	*n.* something used to carry and move people or things *Ex. Cars and buses are vehicles.*
build	*v.* to make something *Ex. They are building a new bridge.*
invent	*v.* to make something for the first time *Ex. When was the camera invented?*
brick	*n.* a hard block of baked clay *Ex. This house was built of red brick.*
control	*v.* to make something work in a particular way *Ex. It controls the temperature in the building.*
narrow	*adj.* not wide; limited in size *Ex. The road was too narrow for two cars.*

 Listening

SUR3-4-07
MP3

A Listen to the dialog and choose the best answer. .MP3 WB 31

1. What is the conversation about?

   a. Cars   b. New books   c. Cool food

2. What is true about the boy?

   a. He likes fast cars very much.

   b. He likes white cars very much.

   c. He likes small cars very much.

3. What is true about the girl?

   a. She likes slow cars very much.

   b. She likes fast cars very much.

   c. She likes white cars very much.

B Listen and write the words you hear. .MP3 WB 32

1. A long _________ ago, animal footprints helped __________.

2. People __________ many useful things.

3. People built strong roads with __________.

4. Finally, people invented cars to __________ on __________.

5. There are __________ different kinds of __________.

11

✳ Vocabulary Review

A What does the underlined word mean in each sentence?

1. People used <u>bricks</u> to make roads.
   a. blocks used for building   b. cars used for building
   c. animals used for building

2. Can you <u>build</u> a house?
   a. to cut things into pieces   b. to divide things in half
   c. to make something

B Choose the one word that best fits each sentence.

1. A long time ago, people ___________ animal footprints.
   a. follow   b. follows   c. followed

2. Many roads were ___________ for many things.
   a. built   b. build   c. building

3. Those roads were very ___________ .
   a. strongly   b. stronger   c. strong

✳ Writing

Put the words in the correct order.

1. on / footprints / left / ground / the / Animals

   ____

2. made / with / roads / They / bricks

   ____

3. The / were / strong / very / roads

   ____

✳ Vocabulary

New words to know

brave
adj. having no fear
Ex. My brother is very brave. He caught a thief.

knight
n. a man who has been given a title of honor by a king
Ex. Sir Lancelot was a famous knight.

iron
n. a strong heavy metal
Ex. Steel is made from iron.

suit
n. a formal set of clothes
Ex. He always wears a suit and tie.

nobleman
n. a man of high rank or title
Ex. The nobleman was famous in his country.

turn
v. to become a particular age; to move
Ex. My son's just turned 18.

protect
v. to keep somebody or something safe
Ex. Parents protect their children.

fight
v. to take part in a war or battle
Ex. They fight for control of the islands.

battle
n. a fight in a war
Ex. He died in battle.

formal
adj. made or done officially
Ex. Don't be so formal.

 Listening

SUR3-5-09
MP3

A Listen to the dialog and choose the best answer. MP3 WB 33

1. What is the conversation about?

   a. The past   b. Knights   c. The present

2. What is true about the conversation?

   a. Knights were very cute.

   b. Knights were very tall.

   c. Knights were very brave.

3. What is true about the boy?

   a. He does not know what a soldier is.

   b. He does not know what a knight is.

   c. He does not know what a picture is.

B Listen and write the words you hear. MP3 WB 34

1. Lots ____________ people wanted to be ____________ .

2. There were ____________ a few noblemen in the past.

3. Fathers ____________ their sons to be ____________ .

4. Knights fought ____________ in ____________ .

5. Iron suits could ____________ knights.

✳ Vocabulary Review

A What does the underlined word mean in each sentence?

1. They were <u>brave</u> people.
   a. doing something in fear
   b. doing something without fear
   c. doing something with pleasure

2. <u>Iron</u> is very useful.
   a. a weak, heavy metal   b. a soft metal
   c. a strong, heavy metal

B Choose the one word that best fits each sentence.

1. A long time ago, knights ___________ horses.
   a. rode   b. rides   c. ride

2. My father taught me to ___________ strong.
   a. is   b. am   c. be

3. Iron suits were used to ___________ knights.
   a. protects   b. protect   c. protected

✳ Writing

Put the words in the correct order.

1. wore / They / and / iron / suits / horses / rode

   ____

2. another / knight / worked / for / He

   ____

3. people / very / Knights / brave / were

   ____

✳ Vocabulary

New words to know

season   *n.* one of the periods of different weather
Ex. The four seasons are spring, summer, autumn and winter.

summer   *n.* the warmest time of the year, between spring and autumn
Ex. We can go swimming in the summer.

autumn   *n.* the time of the year between summer and winter
Ex. I feel lonely in the autumn.

winter   *n.* the coldest time of the year, between autumn and spring
Ex. It snows a lot in the winter here.

ripen   *v.* to become ready to be eaten
Ex. These tomatoes will ripen in two weeks.

air   *n.* the mixture of gases around the earth
Ex. I need some fresh air.

bloom   *v.* to produce flowers
Ex. This flower blooms in May.

change   *v.* to become different
Ex. I changed my mind.

ready   *adj.* prepared; willing
Ex. I will be ready soon.

weather   *n.* the climate at a certain place and time
Ex. What is the weather like there?

 Listening

SUR3-6-11
MP3

A   Listen to the dialog and choose the best answer. MP3 **WB** 35

1. What is the conversation about?

    a. One's favorite season   b. One's favorite shoes

    c. One's favorite clothes

2. What is true about the boy?

    a. He does not enjoy swimming.

    b. He loves snow.

    c. His favorite season is summer.

3. What is true about the girl?

    a. Her favorite season is spring.

    b. She loves snow.

    c. She enjoys swimming.

B   Listen and write the words you hear. MP3 **WB** 36

1. Many people like ___________ flowers.

2. In the summer, ___________ begin to ___________.

3. In the ___________, people see leaves ___________ color.

4. Everything is ___________ in the ___________.

5. Every ___________ is ___________.

✳ Vocabulary Review

A What does the underlined word mean in each sentence?

1. Everybody was <u>quiet</u>.
   a. not noisy   b. very noisy   c. very quick

2. Do these apples begin to <u>ripen</u>?
   a. to become ready to be sold
   b. to become ready to be eaten
   c. to become ready to be bought

B Choose the one word that best fits each sentence.

1. Are you _____________ for the test?
   a. readiness   b. readily   c. ready

2. Flowers begin to _____________.
   a. bloom   b. blooms   c. blooming

3. You can see trees _____________ color at that time of year.
   a. changes   b. changed   c. change

✳ Writing

Put the words in the correct order.

1. to / begin / ripen / Fruits

   ____

2. ready / get / People / for / weather / cold

   ____

3. season / something / has / Every / special

   ____

✳ Vocabulary

New words to know

flag   *n.* a piece of cloth with a pattern
                  Ex. This flag is the symbol of our company.

over   *prep.* more than a particular time, amount, etc.
                  Ex. He's over sixty.

stripe   *n.* a line or long, narrow section
                  Ex. Zebras have black and white stripes.

corner   *n.* a part where two lines or edges meet
                  Ex. Put the lamp in the corner.

star   *n.* a small point of light in the sky at night
                  Ex. The stars were shining.

represent   *v.* to stand for or be a sign of
                  Ex. Doves represent peace.

meaning   *n.* the thing or idea that something represents
                  Ex. This word has two different meanings.

proud   *adj.* feeling pleased and worthy
                  Ex. They are proud of their new house.

upper   *adj.* near or at the top of something
                  *Ex. There is a restaurant on the upper floor of this
                  building.*

worthy   *adj.* good enough for something
                  Ex. It is worthy to pay $20.

 Listening 

SUR3-7-13
MP3

A Listen to the dialog and choose the best answer. MP3 WB 37

1. What is the conversation about?

   a. Stars   b. The American flag

   c. Stripes

2. What is true about the conversation?

   a. The American flag has 15 stars in it.

   b. The American flag has 50 stars in it.

   c. The American flag has no stripes.

3. What is true about the boy?

   a. He knows all about the American flag.

   b. He likes the American flag.

   c. He didn't know the term "Stars and Stripes."

B Listen and write the words you hear. MP3 WB 38

1. We are _______ of our country's flag.

2. The _______ flag is over 200 _______ old.

3. The American _______ has many stars and _______.

4. The upper _______ of the American flag has 50 _______.

5. 50 stars represent 50 _______.

✶ Vocabulary Review

A What does the underlined word mean in each sentence?

1. Some people like <u>stripes</u> so much.
    a. long, narrow bands or lines
    b. long, narrow paths for people
    c. long, narrow paths for animals

2. I am very <u>proud</u> of my father.
    a. feeling angry and mad
    b. feeling unhappy and sad
    c. feeling pleased and worthy

B Choose the one word that best fits each sentence.

1. Every country ____________ important to its people.
    a. are   b. is   c. am
2. We are ____________ of our country.
    a. proud   b. proudly   c. pride
3. The British flag is also ____________ the Union Jack.
    a. calls   b. called   c. call

✶ Writing

Put the words in the correct order.

1. has / country / own / its / Every / flag

    ____

2. flags / All / the / different / are

    ____

3. look / flag / at / American / Let's / the

    ____

✳ Vocabulary

New words to know

policeman	*n.* a man who is a member of a police force *Ex. My uncle is a policeman.*
stand	*v.* to be on your feet *Ex. He was standing near the window.*
door	*n.* an opening for entering or leaving *Ex. Someone is knocking on the door.*
guard	*v.* to keep somebody or something safe *Ex. The building is guarded by two dogs.*
floor	*n.* a level of a building *Ex. Her office is on the second floor.*
president	*n.* the chief leader of a country *Ex. He wanted to be the President of the United States of America.*
love	*v.* to like very much *Ex. I really love swimming.*
much	*adv.* to a great degree *Ex. Thank you very much for the flowers.*
country	*n.* a nation; the territory of a nation *Ex. There are more than 200 countries in the world.*
famous	*adj.* known about by many people in many places *Ex. Many famous people often stay in this hotel.*

 **Listening**

SUR3-8-15
MP3

A Listen to the dialog and choose the best answer.  **WB** 39

1. What is the conversation about?

    a. The President of the United States of America

    b. The White House

    c. A greenhouse

2. What is true about the girl?

    a. She thinks that the White House is amazing.

    b. She does not like the White House.

    c. She does not like the boy.

3. What is true about the conversation?

    a. The boy knows everything about the White House.

    b. The President of Korea lives in the White House.

    c. The girl knows a lot about the White House.

B Listen and write the words you hear. **WB** 40

1. The White _______ is in Washington D.C.

2. Lots of policemen _______ the White House _______ .

3. There are three _______ in the _______ House.

4. The President and _______ family live _______ the second and third floor.

5. The President _______ on the _______ floor.

✳ Vocabulary Review

A   What does the underlined word mean in each sentence?

1.   Sandra <u>always</u> studies music.
      a. often   b. sometimes   c. all the time

2.   Many police officers <u>guard</u> the President of America.
      a. to watch over somebody   b. to hurt somebody
      c. to kick somebody

B   Choose the one word that best fits each sentence.

1.   The President of the United States ____________ about his
      country.
      a. care   b. cares   c. caring

2.   The other rooms ____________ for them.
      a. is   b. are   c. am

3.   You can ____________ the White House from the street.
      a. sees   b. seeing   c. see

✳ Writing

Put the words in the correct order.

1.   the / You / White / can / in / House / see / Washington
      D.C.

      ____

2.   guard / it / and / They / night / day

      ____

3.   House / are / There / the / floors / three / in / White

      ____

✳ Vocabulary

New words to know

hunt	*v.* to try to find and kill *Ex. They needed to hunt deer in order to stay alive.*
berry	*n.* a small, soft fruit with seeds *Ex. Those berries are sweet.*
root	*n.* the part of a plant that is under the ground *Ex. Roots take water from the soil.*
kill	*v.* to make somebody or something die *Ex. She was killed in the plane crash.*
wild	*adj.* living or growing in natural conditions *Ex. This is a wild flower.*
discover	*v.* to find before someone else *Ex. Who did discover America?*
raw	*adj.* not cooked *Ex. Raw vegetables are good for your health.*
raise	*v.* to take care of animals *Ex. You can't raise lions.*
farmer	*n.* a person who works on a farm *Ex. My father is a farmer.*
decide	*v.* to think carefully and choose *Ex. We decided to study hard.*

✳ Listening

SUR3-9-17
MP3

A Listen to the dialog and choose the best answer. 🎵 WB 41

1. What is the conversation about?

   a. Fishing   b. Boys   c. Girls

2. What is true about the boy?

   a. He enjoys fishing.

   b. He does not like fishing.

   c. He thinks that fishing is cool.

3. What is true about the girl?

   a. She does not know anything about the past.

   b. She knows a lot about the past.

   c. She does not like fishing.

B Listen and write the words you hear. 🎵 WB 42

1. In the past, people _________ for ________.

2. ________ killed ________ animals.

3. People ________ fire to ________ food.

4. People learned ________ to ________ animals.

5. There were ________ people to ________.

✱ Vocabulary Review

A What does the underlined word mean in each sentence?

1. Many people like <u>raw</u> fish.
    a. not hot   b. not cold   c. not cooked

2. People <u>raise</u> pigs to eat.
    a. to take part in   b. to take care of
    c. to take a nap

B Choose the one word that best fits each sentence.

1. In the past, people ___________ wild animals.
    a. killed   b. kills   c. kill

2. People learned how to ___________ food.
    a. cooked   b. cook   c. cooks

3. Towns began to ___________ .
    a. grew   b. grows   c. grow

✱ Writing

Put the words in the correct order.

1. time / ago / hunted / A / people / food / long / for

    ____

2. food / raw / ate / they / the / Instead / all

    ____

3. people / farmers / became / Some

    ____

✳ Vocabulary

New words to know

ocean	*n.* the largest bodies of water on the earth *Ex. Two thirds of the earth's surface is covered by ocean.*
level	*n.* the height; the amount *Ex. He plays tennis at a high level.*
movement	*n.* an act of moving *Ex. I could see some movement.*
tide	*n.* the regular change in the level of the sea or ocean *Ex. The tide is coming in.*
land	*n.* the solid part of the surface of the earth *Ex. She owns lots of land.*
beach	*n.* an area of sand beside the sea *Ex. I will sit on the beach.*
soon	*adv.* in a short time from now *Ex. He left soon after me.*
show	*v.* to let somebody see *Ex. I showed the letter to him.*
wonder	*v.* to feel surprise *Ex. I wonder at his ability.*
surprise	*n.* something not expected *Ex. To my surprise, they are all kind.*

 Listening

SUR3-10-19
MP3

A Listen to the dialog and choose the best answer. MP3 **WB** 43

1. What is the conversation about?

    a. Swimming   b. The ocean   c. A horse

2. What is true about the boy?

    a. He does not like to swim in the ocean.

    b. He thinks that the ocean is very dirty.

    c. He likes to swim in the ocean.

3. What is true about the girl?

    a. She thinks that the ocean is very dirty.

    b. She thinks that the ocean is interesting.

    c. She thinks that the boy is foolish.

B Listen and write the words you hear. MP3 **WB** 44

1. The ocean _______ all the _______ .

2. Many people like to _______ in the _______ .

3. People can _______ lots of things on the _______ .

4. The _______ by the _______ is not very deep.

5. High _______ will come again soon.

✳ Vocabulary Review

A What does the underlined word mean in each sentence?

1. Do not swim at high <u>tide</u>.
    a. change in the level of a mountain
    b. change in the level of a building
    c. change in the level of the sea
2. Look at the <u>movement</u> of the sea.
    a. something that remains the same
    b. something that changes position
    c. something that does not move

B Choose the one word that best fits each sentence.

1. At high tide, people like to ___________.
    a. fishing   b. fish   c. fishes
2. The water is not ___________.
    a. deep   b. deeply   c. depth
3. The tide will ___________ in soon.
    a. came   b. comes   c. come

✳ Writing

Put the words in the correct order.

1. ocean / changes / all / of / the / time / The / the / level

____

2. high / like / during / People / tide / to / fish

____

3. soon / tide / come / High / again / will

____

✳ Vocabulary

New words to know

future	*n.* time that is yet to come
	Ex. Don't be afraid of what future will hold.
main	*adj.* most important
	Ex. The main road is always busy.
store	*v.* to keep something
	Ex. I store my books in a box.
trunk	*n.* the thick central part of a tree
	Ex. The branches grow from the trunk.
send	*v.* to make something go to another place
	Ex. Don't forget to send me a postcard.
branch	*n.* one of the main parts of a tree
	Ex. Those branches are strong.
twig	*n.* a small, thin branch on a tree
	Ex. The twig was broken.
bark	*n.* the hard outer covering of a tree
	Ex. This bark is very thick and hard.
bud	*n.* a small lump on a tree that develops into a flower
	Ex. Be careful not to hurt the bud!
lump	*n.* a bump or swelling
	Ex. I had a lump on my forehead.

✴ Listening

A Listen to the dialog and choose the best answer. 🎵 WB 45

1. What is the conversation about?

    a. Elephants   b. Dogs

    c. All the parts of a tree

2. What is true about the boy?

    a. He knows everything about trees.

    b. He does not know much about trees.

    c. He likes trees very much.

3. What is true about the conversation?

    a. A tree has five different parts.

    b. A tree has three different parts.

    c. The boy likes the girl.

B Listen and write the words you hear. 🎵 WB 46

1. ________ part of a tree is ________ important.

2. Different ________ have different ________ .

3. The ________ hold water and ________ food.

4. The ________ sends water ________ to the leaves.

5. All ________ parts help each ________ .

 Vocabulary Review

A What does the underlined word mean in each sentence?

1. People <u>send</u> many things through the mail.
    a. to make something remain the same
    b. to make something go to another place
    c. to make something smaller

2. We need to <u>store</u> some food.
    a. to keep something   b. to remove something
    c. to put something away

B Choose the one word that best fits each sentence.

1. Each part ___________ an important job.
    a. have   b. having   c. has

2. The bark of a tree ___________ hard.
    a. are   b. is   c. am

3. The branches of a tree ___________ very important.
    a. are   b. is   c. am

 Writing

Put the words in the correct order.

1. main / A / parts / has / tree / five

    ____

2. has / special / part / Each / job / a

    ____

3. also / buds / The / are / important / very

    ____

✳ Vocabulary

New words to know

seed   *n.* a small, hard part of a plant from which new plants grow
Ex. I bought a packet of sunflower seeds.

other   *pron.* the additional one
Ex. There are others in my room.

slowly   *adv.* at a slow speed; not quickly
Ex. He walked slowly along the street.

grow   *v.* to increase in size or number
Ex. Plants grow from seeds.

eat   *v.* to put food into your mouth
Ex. Who ate all the cookies?

must   *auxil.* used for saying that it is necessary
Ex. I must go home now.

sunlight   *n.* the light from the sun
Ex. Plants need sunlight to grow.

so   *conj.* with the result that
Ex. She felt tired, so she went to bed.

carry   *v.* to hold something while moving
Ex. Would you help carry these boxes?

quickly   *adv.* fast or hurriedly
Ex. He is running quickly.

 Listening

SUR3-12-23
MP3

A Listen to the dialog and choose the best answer.  WB 47

1. What is the conversation about?

a. The sun   b. Seeds   c. Wind

2. What is true about the girl?

a. She knows everything about seeds.

b. She thinks that trees are beautiful.

c. She wonders how seeds become plants.

3. What is true about the conversation?

a. Seeds cannot become big trees.

b. Sunlight does not help seeds grow.

c. To become plants, seeds need water and sunlight.

B Listen and write the words you hear. WB 48

1. ___________ have many different ___________.

2. ___________ carries seeds to other places.

3. Water and ___________ help seeds ___________ well.

4. To grow well, seeds ___________ have water and sunlight.

5. Animals ___________ seeds that fall on the ___________.

✴ Vocabulary Review

A What does the underlined word mean in each sentence?

1. Would you like to <u>carry</u> the box to my room?
    a. to remove something while walking
    b. to hold something while moving
    c. to erase something while writing

2. Be careful! Drive <u>slowly</u>.
    a. at high speed   b. at full speed
    c. at a slow speed

B Choose the one word that best fits each sentence.

1. Seeds are starting to ___________.
    a. grows   b. growing   c. grow

2. When they ___________ water, they are happy.
    a. getting   b. get   c. gets

3. We must ___________ the room.
    a. cleans   b. clean   c. cleaning

✴ Writing

Put the words in the correct order.

1. different / Seeds / sizes / have

   ____

2. big / are / others / small / and / are / Some

   ____

3. grow / quickly / seeds / Some

   ____

StartUp Reading 3

Workbook